21ˢᵗ CENTURY THINKS

500 ORIGINAL THOUGHTS OF A COMMON MAN

THANKS SCATTY ANN

A big thanks to Scatty Ann 'The potty one by the pier' who truly embraced the first edition in the veracious spirit that I had willed, energising the creative forces with her unparalleled buoyancy, enthusiasm, curiosity and good cheer!

Thank you for being you!

FRONT COVER ART

The front cover artwork is a digital rework of an oil painting I did in 1989 called 'Broken'.

AUTHOR'S NOTE

When I refer to 'here' or 'this country' I am referring to France where I currently live.

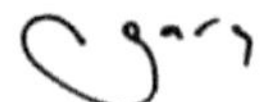

21ˢᵗ CENTURY THINKS

500 ORIGINAL THOUGHTS OF A COMMON MAN

THE QUOTE TALES II

GARY BRYON PATEMAN

ISBN 978-2-492423-00-0

Original Artwork: Gary Bryon Pateman

DEATH

A life well lived leads
to a death well
died.

In the blink of an eye I
remembered the day I
was born as the rope
bit down on the
branch.

When I die I hope that
my children will have loved
me enough to cry over their
cornflakes, but not so much
that it spoils their lunch.

It is the sole privilege of the
condemned to rise
above the truth.

Many American deaths begin
with a shooting
pain.

The fanfare, the marching
band, cheering crowds lined
the streets throwing hats
into the air, was it really all
for me, really...? Then the
first shovelful of earth
hit the lid.

I'm so low that I can't even
find a suitable beach
to get washed
up on.

Does the ice crack to warn
us of our impending
doom?

The end, a fractional
acceleration followed
by shortness of
breath under
a diabolical
sky.

The gentle rocking back
and forth obscures the
carnage, sombre yet
desperate, moments
before the stool
flips to one side.

Dress up every day as if
you're attending your
own funeral.

I advise 'instant death' to be
taken a bit more
seriously.

Unhanging the wrongly
convicted. When in
doubt, string 'em
down.

I would like to read my own
posthumous eulogy but fear
that I might just miss the
chance by a day or two.

Bury them below the earth
then look up to the sky
to connect with
them.

Death dredges flippancy
and fancy, exposing
ones vulnerable and
desperately sober spirit.

When I die, someone
promise to tell me as I'm
not sure I'd notice
living here.

Refugees are not statistics,
no matter how many or
by which manner
they perish.

If my imaginary friend
refuses to come to
my funeral then
neither will I.

Think of the forever before
you existed and the forever
once you're gone and now
think how you can maximise
the bit in the middle.

I think the suicide note will
simply read 'it didn't
get better'.

When the time comes,
I hope my shadow will
reassuringly pat me on the
back, take me by the hand
and lead me peacefully
back into the void of
non existence.

I intend to go out in a
blaze of obscurity.

I hope I'll be remembered
as a kind soul with a wicked
sense of humour. Rather than...

The beginning of the
end begins with
perfection.

Is the life of a human the
blink of an eye, the yearning
to be found or a single tear
dense enough to
drown in?

When I've totally lost faith
in the man in the mirror
I will step down and
tip toe away.

When I die, if you wish to
vividly remember some of
our moments together,
play 'Alleluia, Behold the
Bridegroom' by The St
Petersburg Chamber Choir,
close your eyes, don't be
ashamed to drift off
because before you do,
we will be together again.

What more could one
possibly want, than to have
lived both a charming
and charmed life?

Life is a joke and death is the punchline, if you don't get it, just move along, nothing to see here...

When the play 'Gary Bryon Pateman' finally draws to a close either due to a lack of interest, lack of funds, lack of theatre or lack of leading role, please forgive him for having luckily missed 'being booed off stage' by just a few seconds.

One day my heart will have
had enough, down tools and
refuse to pump another
solitary droplet and
I know in my heart
of hearts, that
consciousness
will be obliged
to follow.

Life is learning one's lines as
one goes along so as not to
mess up catastrophically.
Death is messing up
catastrophically.

PEOPLE

Since forever, the ego of
man has fouled the
precision of his
judgement.

Like mother to child, only
the locals are permitted to
pillory their paddocks
and pasturelands.

Some people can afford
better principles than
others.

The radiant charm of
another can leave one in
awe, and others in pieces.

Those with visible faults
and evident foibles are so
much more endearing than
those who successfully
camouflage them.

Eventually the downtrodden,
tread downer than
their treaders.

Internet dating is revealing
the secret of a magic trick
before it has been
performed.

Americans who shout
the loudest should
whisper the
quietest.

Her secret submissive life
as a surrogate
salt lick.

Ladies, distance yourselves from men who seek virgins as possessions, exclusivities and who triumph the lack of sexual experiences to be compared against.

Whilst being profoundly scrutinised, his virtues were impeccable.

The little unremarkable public of this huge remarkable republic.

He's as cost conscious as a
10 watt light bulb and
eminently as
dull.

Tragically some
browbeaten women
are bullied to the point of
needing to feel inadequate
to feel anything at all.

Fizzy drinks and crisps are
a blight on Blighty's
blighters.

I know people who
scurry away and bury
reassurances in the hope
of preventing new, contrary
evidence from surfacing.

They wind each other up with
all the pep and punch of
a perfectly sane
cuckoo clock.

One shouldn't take
generosity as
'given'.

First we must understand
where somebody comes
from to truly understand
why they are where they
are now and where they
are likely to be going.

Like a two year old who's
first learned to say 'No',
they will defend their
opinion to the death,
even in the face of
contrary evidence
like truth, facts
and verity.

Unfortunately they
appear to suffer from
a manifestation of
inconsideration.

As a foreigner, the minimum
one pays is the maximum
and the maximum one
gets is the minimum.

Displaying ones trophies is
patting oneself on the back
using other people's
hands.

Blundering dullardic types
passionately ridiculing
themselves with their
ill perceived, misspelt,
fist thumping blunt
monosyllabic
promulgations.

The profundity of his
principles was directly
paradoxical to the
commitment he was
prepared to invest
in them.

Few can imagine what's
in the minds of
others.

While masking what they
really mean, when someone
says 'Oh that's far too
clever for me', it
probably is.

Here, if the truth doesn't
align with their belief,
they change the
truth, not their
belief.

Foolishly foolish fools fool
themselves that their
opinion is the only
one worth
listening
to.

Those who blatantly lie
to ones face, are obviously
unaware of the consequences
of such an act, the painfully
slow, silent unravelling of
respect to such an
undignified
deed.

They were a couple who
spent their lives chasing other
people's dreams, occasionally
getting close enough to
catch a blakey to
the gums.

Those of that particular
persuasion are bound
and bonded by
BDSM.

So overweight he was
considered more of
a gathering.

REFLECTIONS

Compiling this book of wisdom hasn't made me wiser, just better at compiling.

Pride is a blind man claiming that his eyes see the furthest because he's unwilling to acknowledge that others still possess sight.

I have become spiritually tactile and physically theoretical.

Every single choice we
make says something about
who we are, add them all
together and that *is*
who we are.

Social media; the more we
know about everyone,
the less we know
about anyone.

All that glitters is either
gold, grit or gary, be careful
what you wish for...

Reflection is the drum of
fingernails on a porcelain
tea cup while contemplating
the depth to which one
might be in love.

Anxious of deserting the
chaos for fear it may
unmask yet more chaos.

I guess if I was a little
less odd, I'd have more of
an idea where 'within the
confines of the pale' ends
and 'beyond it' begins.

There is no such thing as
absolute silence for even
'listening' possesses
its own sound.

A distant rumble of thunder
at a picnic should only be a
cause for concern depending
on which way the wind
is blowing.

This country welcomes
immigrants as fly paper
welcomes flies.

My mantra is 'think progressively, remain intellectually humble', my whimsy is 'bum, tit & willy'.

Contrary to what one may believe, life for the majority is simply 'painting by numbers'.

Assume that your opinion is simply the best that you've 'yet heard' and not the best 'ever heard'.

If something is worn
naturally and with
independence of mind,
it will always fit.

Quirky is charming,
freaky is not.

The sweet meat stench,
constant hum of neurone
activity and clitter clatter of
ideas, bleary eyed, stumbling
chaotically into the
daylight.

The antidote for those
blinded by certitude
is humility.

The confinement of icy
politeness is starved of the
earthiness of having
toiled in the soil.

Give me the honest reason
which sticks in the craw,
not the dishonest excuse
that's pawing at my
conscience.

Only men bite off as much
toast as possible with
the first mouthful.

'Ethnic cleansing' sounds
like a warm bath, sprinkled
with Tibetan salts, zen candles,
bamboo pipe music and a
long calming soak...
But it isn't.

I hypnotised myself into
thinking that I've never
been hypnotised, so...

Administered with deft,
stealth and patience, silence
can be ultimately
damning.

This countries inbred
nepotism limits its vision
of the world to no further
than its own frontiers.

Getting drunk in another
language is like scratching
an itch with somebody
else's fingers nails.

Our dreams, no matter how
ludicrous in hindsight, were
as unquestionably real as
this very moment.

Here, reality is distorted to
fit with their emotionally
driven interpretation of it.

Being amongst ones
favourite things is to
drop anchor in a place
where one truly
belongs.

An unhealthy respect for
authority shows an
unhealthy respect
for one's
self.

Trying to inject fresh ideas
from outside of one's own
consciousness is like
imagining what's
on the other side
of an infinite
universe.

I don't think,
therefore
I isn't.

I resist trends for 'trends sake', fashion for 'fashions sake' and modernity for 'modernity's sake' which helps explain why I can appear contemporarily irrelevant.

Original Artwork © Gary Bryon Pateman

SUCCESS

Self belief is a trampette
which occasionally
propels one in an
unexpected
direction.

Too many otherwise decent
people lick their way
to the top.

Success is happiness when it
includes the manner with
which you got
there.

We could improve society
in an instant if we taught
curiosity and inquisitiveness.

Success is coming in second
after anticipating coming
in third.

The most comprehensive
solution for the greater
good can usually be
found bookended
by opposing
views.

A 'true home' run is
successfully boiling an
egg to somebody
else's liking.

Unfortunately 'little man
syndrome' applies to men
of all shapes and sizes.

A man's self-aggrandised
perspective of his own
success, often evaporates
where it meets fresh air.

One is condemned if
unsuccessful and utterly
condemned if successful.

Why limit oneself to what
one knows one
can do.

The medals around the neck
of the hypercompetitive
come at a greater
cost than just
sacrifice.

Corporate success is all
tongues, bums and the
abandonment of
dignity.

Success is going to bed a
better person than when
you woke up.

I'm undecided if success
is looking in the mirror and
feeling pleased with what
one sees or not giving
a damn.

Succeed by the measure of
one's own failures and not
the successes of
others.

To truly embrace the
beauty of the rose,
one must first,
be prepared
to bleed.

Success to the inadequate is
simply possessing more
stuff than others.

President Chump, a man
who rose, aided, from the
depths of privilege to
foster even more
entitlement.

A modicum of intelligence
can be a dangerous
thing inside the
wrong head.

Is it a blessing or a burden
to realise one's
limitations?

Is success the pieces
of silver, or the manner
with which they were
acquired?

Trying to prove that one
isn't a 'small man' is the
only proof necessary,
that one is indeed,
a 'small man'.

The impenetrable
thraldom of
'if only...'

Being superhuman isn't
simply picking up the
heaviest rock on the
beach, it's successfully
surveying the sand
beneath ones feet.

From rags to more rags.

Success is doing anything
other than what I've
been doing for
the last
5 years.

Fame for fame's sake is
worthless recognition
for a journey as yet
to be undertaken.

Success is finishing what
one didn't think could
be finished.

The only truly successful
man is he who compares
himself not against
others.

Failure is contextual; one
may have failed to get
to the airport on time,
but successfully avoided
boarding a plane that
fell out of the sky.

To succeed is to have first
failed, and then put a
generous helping of
distance between
that experience
and whatever
happens
next.

If I successfully tied a
knot and was awarded a
proficiency badge by the
scouts or I unsuccessfully
tied a knot and failed to
hang myself, which
should I be most
proud of…?

Isn't 'success' simply
'amelioration' whatever one's
circumstances, rather than
a predetermined bar
set at a fixed
height?

Original Artwork © Gary Bryon Pateman

RELATIONSHIPS

Our fiercest of enemies
were once our closest
of friends.

My partner attended
a course on how to cure
her contradictory nature.
Oh, apparently she
didn't.

Singularitively speaking,
she drives me
bonka.

She was as affectionate
as a dysfunctional
Kevlar vest.

We evidently derive from
different solar systems
but by proximity happen
to share the occasional
pocket of air.

Opium, I'm your closest,
most loyal
fiend.

Relationships often suffer
from subsidence.

Friendship is doing the
things you really don't
want to with the grace of
appearing as if there's
nothing you'd rather
be doing.

Seven years ago I don't
remember breaking a
mirror the day I met
my partner?

She scrubs and polishes
desperately trying to
remove the stain
of a difficult
childhood.

As the host, she seeks
conflict as a headache
seeks a head.

Your partner's blood hasn't
actually run cold, perhaps
you've just lost sense of
how to warm it up.

Seeing an ex-lover is the
same as seeing a star in the
night sky, clearly it's visible
but in reality it has long
since died, leaving only
a mirage of what once
was, but is no
longer.

When the boy King's crown
slipped and his shortcomings
laid bare, he'd replace those
closest, with others, to whom
he could once again feel
superior to.

She has an unerring eye to
uncover problems that
aren't there.

She was sympathetically
armoured coated and
benevolently astute
with foibles that
could blunt
razor-wire.

Up until I made their wives
laugh too loudly, I had
many friends here.

Even if a door is left ajar
but never entered, at
least it isn't shut.

Whether a friend eagerly
orders my book or hangs
back hoping to be given one,
says a lot about the friend.
Whether I give them one or
not says a lot about me.

She was as intimate
as an airport
lounge.

Don't be foolish enough to
think you know the status of
someone's relationship.

Bound by loyalty, nagged
by injustice, sealed by
friendship.

Some focus their energies,
making special efforts to
find fault with others, but
keep tripping over the fact
that the faults they claim
to find, mirror their own.

She lurches from one
conflict to another like a
dance floor drunkard
at a wedding.

If one is diagnosed with
tedium, take 'Life' every
day until its expiry date.

Even with a herculean effort
she can barely suppress the
rage and exaggerated
self imposed sense
of injustice.

Women nearly always make
wiser choices than men,
except when it comes
to choosing
men.

If your day job is moaning
then snoring covers
the night shift
as well.

Emotionless, eyes as cold
as steel, the puckered
stance of love
lost.

Her demeanour was as
foreboding as a freshly
dredged reservoir.

Even the admiral of the
galleon is somebody
else's slave.

She is so contradictory
that in order for us agree
with each other, I've started
saying the opposite of what
I actually think, unfortunately
since she found out,
so has she.

The wearing of earplugs
while sleeping next to
someone who snores is like
wearing a peg on ones nose
while sleeping next to a
rotting corpse, cover up
as we may, we can't fool
ourselves that easily.

One's ears owe it to one's
intellect to listen, one's eyes
owe it to one's vision to see,
one's brain owes it to one's
wisdom to learn and one's
mouth owes it to one's
voice to rebuke injustice.

Original Artwork: Gary Bryon Pateman

POLITICS

Some politician's speeches
give you goose bumps and
make your hair lay flat,
lank and lifeless.

A career politician bears the
scars of compromise and
hypocrisy like a priest's
confession.

Many politicians begin
ethically sound yet
finish unethically
silent.

Conviction applied liberally
is more convincing than
conviction free from
doubt or scrutiny.

A good politician should be
stuffed, mounted on the
wall and then dusted
not very often.

Anyone else see a problem
with the politicians mantra;
'We have to be seen to be...'

Trying to decide who'll
be the next American
democratic presidential
candidate is like picking
the bones out of
a caucus.

The current Labour Party is
so full of huff, puff, bluster
and bigotry that it resembles
a bitter 'n' twisted old widow
who despises everyone,
but none so much
as herself.

Saint Ruggler of the
Unwelfare State.

A corrupt politician is made
of blue asbestos with a
government health
warning sewn into
every falsehood.

Lying, boondoggling and
cunning are often the first
apparatus to be found in
a politician's toolbox.

Presidents lie in state
before and after they die.

This government allows
protestations in the streets.
If they didn't, there would
be protestations in the
streets.

I think in order to keep them
honest, politicians should
have a view of the gallows
from their office
window.

Listening with an open
mind has been temporarily
suspended until political
correctness stops sulking
and welcomes back
common sense with
open arms.

Political correctness hangs
menacingly above us like
an open noose eager to
suspend even the most
meek and mild if they
stray from the belief
of the hangman.

Modern political correctness
is scrutinising the past to
punish people for something
that wasn't even considered
inappropriate during
the period when it
was done.

Sadly during the national
Brexit negotiations, my
beloved *Auntie got
in a muddle and
became terribly
undemocratic.
*BBC

Career politicians should
always have a choice,
run the gauntlet
or walk the
plank.

Skilled politicians are
capable of lying through
other people's teeth.

In Europe the stupid
'far right' have risen again
thanks to the stupidity
of the 'far left'.

People voted
conservative because they
are considerably closer to
the centre than the current
Labour Party and therefore
closer to the Labour Party
that they'd previously
voted for.

Here, everybody is
president of something
meaning that nobody
is actually a president
of anything.

It's part of a politicians
remit to ransack the mouths
of others whose opinions
are superior to
theirs.

The 'remain or leave' Brexit
fence lies in splinters having
been pushed, pulled, kicked
and shoved back and forth,
it also happened to be
where I used to sit,
all but alone.

I've attended political rallies
where the participants are
all but on the point of
climax at the drone
of their own
verbosity.

When a political party seeks
a new leader, suddenly the
hidden ego's rise to the
surface of even the
mildest, Marxist,
knitted tank top
do-gooder.

Politicians, hold your hands
up and apologise, then put
your hands back in your
own pockets and
don't do it
again.

A politician is as
aesthetically pleasing
as a bunion and as
charismatic as the
toe it's currently
clinging to.

The government picks our
pockets and then decides
how much of our money
they can afford
to give us
back.

By dint of ambition
and compromise, career
politicians with a virtuous
vision lose sight of where
their original ethical
compass pointed.

Politician's dentures continue
to chatter long after they've
been removed for the night.

Politicians will always help
the public by laying their
coats across puddles
that aren't there.

Some politicians send a
shiver down a spine just as
a spine can send a shiver
down a politician.

TIME

I feel for the future as an
amputee feels pain in the
foot that has been
removed.

I cannot dance in either
Heaven or Hell, so I
guess I'm stuck being
a limbo dancer.

With fading memory I'm not
so much 'the thinker' as
'the thoughter'.

At my age, my preferred
choice of exercise is digging
a large hole, that way, when
I drop down dead, my
nearest and dearest
can just fill
it in.

I've lived most of my life on
the other side of the mirror
where everything's
backward and
the other way
round.

Do you believe in the
hereafter or the
therebeforer?

Social justice warriors will
scrutinise your past, to
judge your present, to
destroy your future.

What is time but a linear
tube perpetually morphing
itself in tandem with
our existence?

The cast of my shadow
bestows grace upon an
otherwise distorted
form.

Is not every period of time
considered to be the most
relevant by those living
through it?

Concerning the sands of
time, my hourglass is
neither half full nor
half empty.

Age is beckoning me into a
comfy armchair adorned
with a couple of laced
doilies and a discretely
hidden whoopee
cushion.

The 'present' never really
exists as, ad infinitum, the
future instantly becomes
the present which
instantly becomes
the past.

Endless days of nothingness
drift into one long billowing
sheet of obscurity.

My old age aspirations
consist of sitting on the
terrace wearing olive,
tweed, urine stained
trousers, smoking an
utterly inappropriate
oriental ivory pipe and
swearing at the birds
as they enter my
airspace.

Thrashing out the age of
insanity in constant conflict
with the furrowed browsers.

With age I tend to lurch from
one forgettable year to the
next without breaking
stride.

All roads from whence
spawned lead to whom,
what and where we are
in this moment...

The blank canvas of life has
aged, yellowed and repels
spontaneous hues of
the vibrancy of youth
for a politer, quieter
palette, less likely
to ruffle.

With age, my life options
have become a case of
drawing straws, there's
short, shorter still and
'is that even a straw?'

As age tiptoes closer,
success isn't running the
4 minute mile, or even
running for 4 minutes,
it's doing anything
for 4 minutes without
creaking, squeaking
or leaking.

Is the rapidity of life altered
whether one's mind is
tidy and organised
or messy and
chaotic?

We are fascinated by the
future, seduced by the
past and impervious to the
present. Which is curious
when one considers that
we are only ever alive
in the present.

The true value of life is
equal amongst all, however
the potential for it to
flourish depends on
how one defines
fulfilment.

An apparently 'more approachable appearance' has led to tourists trusting me with their cameras to take family photos. I must have misplaced my rebellious edginess.

If a mayfly lives the full 24 hours, its life has been as full, rich and meaningful as one who is expecting a letter from the queen.

Live your life as if you have
all the time in the world
or none at all.

As an older man I tend to
'keep off the grass' not to
avoid damaging it but to
avoid feeling paranoid.

We will rue the day that we
are capable of making a
chain that cannot
be broken.

As an adolescent I could often be found urban grazing, unwittingly attending the street scholarity of meagre yearnings and ill ambitioned wretchedness.

As age slowly got the better of him, his idea of exercise was to break into a sweat putting on a track suit.

The judge and jury for
disagreements has always
been 'evidence', assembled
with facts, driven by truth.
Currently its 'emotion',
assembled with assumption
and driven by hysteria.

We owe a debt to use
our brain that must
be settled from
time to time.

Original Artwork © Gary Bryon Pateman

UTTERANCES

The burglars around here
lack confidence so I've
had an insecurity
alarm fitted.

She loved her country like
a perverted uncle whose
fortune she stood
to inherit.

Agricultural intellect
discerns that the red tractor
doesn't go faster than
the blue one simply
because it's red.

Ballet coaches tend to keep
their students on
their toes.

It is almost exclusively the
envious, spiritually bereft
and socially emulous who
seek to besmirch the
noble, generous
of heart.

Only move abroad if you
were already at the bottom
of the list of invitees in your
country of origin.

I've currently got Bell's
palsy on both sides of my
face. I now have to tuck
my chin into the front
of my trousers.

One could pluck a musical
note from the white noise
created by pleading
while mute.

Those born miserable
surround themselves with
chaos to equate their
perpetual discontentment.

At Sunday school I was
punished for being the only
one who didn't close his eyes
during prayer. Anyone else
see a problem here...?

It's logical that you believe
you have the best opinion;
it's logical to believe that
you don't have the
best opinion.

At the earth's core, does
gravity pull outwards or
inwards in every direction?

Isolation renders one
unrecognisable in reflection,
sense and habit, marked by
the slow untethering of
self-consciousness.

The most worrying thing is
that I'm exactly who you
think I am, and
so am I.

I've become an innocent
bystander in my
own life.

If you feel that you live
in an area full of scum, in a
road inhabited by scum and
live next door to scum, take
a look at who's sitting next
to you on the sofa and then
in the mirror... Yep.

I am my own imaginary
friend... and enemy.

This country suffers from
an epidemic of couldn't
carelessness.

My self perception is not
dissimilar to the goldfish,
whose only image of itself,
is in the distorted
reflection of a
fish bowl.

As one fills up ones 'room
to improve' it obviously
empties the more
it fills up.

Some will disagree profusely
with themselves.

When that feeling
that 'somebody's watching
you' turns out to be true, is
it intuition or do we forget
all the times when nobody
was there?

The man who seeks to please
everyone, is to himself,
a traitor.

Simply being honest doesn't
define you, only those
who are not.

I've spent my whole life
mimicking myself, and
I'm even starting to
look like me.

I'm so poor that if I sold my
liver to buy some tripe, it'd
be offal and I wouldn't
kidney body
about it.

Is one to blame when one
doesn't even know that one
should know better.

There is an infinite stream
of lies from which to choose
from, selecting the most
appropriate one at the right
time and making it sound
credible is what separates
the chaff from the wheat.

The suspicious minded
are often arrogant for they
suspect everything, so when
the genuine reason surfaces,
they selectively remember
solely that particular
suspicion.

Why assault me with your views when with a bit more class and charisma you could caress and nurture me into your way of thinking?

One is less likely to recapture lost love than arm wrestle the Venus de Milo.

I hope this book is easy to pick up and difficult to put down. Rather than...

While causality points in
different directions yet
almost meets full circle,
complete freedom and
totalitarianism almost
glance behinds.

Does the actual sky occupy
the space outside of all the
silhouettes of civilisation
and nature or does any
of it begin beneath
the roofs of the
many?

Original Artwork© Gary Bryon Pateman

WORK

Work is existentially harder
when one doesn't
have any.

I can put up with shovelling
sh*t all day long but I draw
the line at having to ask
to go and have one.

Perhaps unsurprisingly
the shoe menders
convention turned
out to be a load
of cobblers.

Dutch cheesemakers let their cheese mature longer for the grater gouda.

Where I live, an arranged marriage is to wed the boy who owns the tractor.

My ideal job would be screen printing my own designs, publishing my own books and someone other than my Mum, buying them.

A 'blessing in disguise' is a
nun giving a benediction
dressed as a priest.

The most difficult job in the
world must be thinking
up original titles for
pornographic
video clips.

I've always wanted to
combine my two passions
of milliner and restaurateur
and if it doesn't work
I'll eat my hat.

Anticipation can be a
wonderful thing, though in
the proximity of a dentist's
waiting room it seems
to carry its own
punishment.

If I was rich I'd hire a chef
to cook healthily for me
and an athlete to go
jogging for me.

I'm too old to do this and
too skint not to.

Today, consecration of the bread and wine will be performed by the priest's alter
ego.

The steps of the corporate ladder are greased with falsehoods, dishonesty and treachery, and that's just the first rung of the wrong ladder they've deliberately sent
you up.

Upstanding, erect,
self-righteous priests, lie
and defile while cruelling
about on all fours.

The taxman has a
demeanour like a leaking
gas tap and a politeness
that belies the savagery
concealed therein.

If possible, avoid
mentioning 'floaters'
during job interviews.

Uglying up beautiful
actresses affords renewed
credibility to their
acting talents.

That company who
manufactured those
inaccurate rulers has
decided to adopt a more
measured approach.

The knack of surviving
repetitive, manual work
is to separate mind
and body.

Speaking from experience,
freelance workers find the
temptation to sexually
harass themselves a
constant distraction.

I'm convinced that there'd
be a lot less anxiety if the
noise of the dentist's
drill sounded like
Mary Poppins.

Escapologists are bound
to escape.

It's worth reminding the
surgeon that the piece of
meat he's about to work
on does in fact belong
to you and you're
pretty keen
on it.

The world is full of mean
spirited individuals who
attempt to scupper the
generous hearted and
relieve them of their
good nature.

Happiness is the time off between leaving your last job and beginning a better one.

My level of basic arithmetic can be easily summed up in one word, 'pretty poor'.

Muddy shoes don't necessarily indicate hard work, perhaps just the wrong choice of footwear.

When an unscrupulous boss
cracks a joke, the less the
browbeaten workforces
understand, the harder
they feel obliged
to laugh.

The moody sky looks like
it's waiting outside the
headmaster's office
having been
up to no
good.

Middle management is the
temptation to smudge your
own, still wet signature,
having just signed on
the dotted line for
a vasectomy.

There must be something
in that Chinese massage
therapy, the other day I
scratched the bottom
of my foot and my
ears waggled.

HAPPINESS

Pure happiness is a silver
fountain pen, black ink and
suitably receptive
parchment.

Achievement is helping ones
children towards happiness.
Accomplishment is your
happiness once they
get there.

A tear can be one of sorrow
or happiness as pain can be
one of hurt or love.

I had so much joy that I
invested some, a few weeks
later I cashed in euphoria
and spent the rest of the
month beside myself.

Another disadvantage of
wearing a mask is that we
don't get to see those
who rarely smile.

To be in love is to be the
freest prisoner in
the world.

A thimbleful of home-grown
mellows even the most
abrasive of dispositions.

Happiness gets its hat and
coat when misery arrives
unannounced and puts
its feet up.

The intrigue of never fully
understanding the one
that you love can be
an intoxicating
fragrance.

An enemy I once considered,
picked a dandelion, unaware
he wasn't alone, lifted it to
the sky and blew softly, and
in this moment I became
overwhelmed with regret,
and learned love for those
that were beyond my
comprehension.

Happiness is inhaling the
fragrance of care and
consideration, not the
reek of neglect and
carelessness.

Happiness is unexpected
amelioration.

The sheer wonderment
of the Hubble telescope
images leave me tearful,
breathless and searching
for an emotion worthy
of such astonishment.

Happiness is forgetting to
check if somebody
has secured the
safety net.

Surely 'Living happily ever
after' should've at least
started by now...?

The last time I dined out with
vengeance, the maitre d'
had to take a few minutes
to compose himself.

I was so extraordinarily
happy once, perhaps I
should have used it more
sparingly, kept some
by for a rainy day.

The shortest shelf life is
when happiness is derived
from the misfortune
of others.

Kindness affords reassurance
and disappointment, love
affords happiness
and pain.

Our personal ambitions
shouldn't only be to change
from unkind to kind, but
from kind to kinder still.

First to sixth Heavens
are 'Predictability', seventh
Heaven is 'Spontaneity',
eighth heaven is doing
something so 'staggeringly
inappropriately regretfully
fun' that ones toes curl
up the wrong way.

Although she successfully
travelled the furthest, she
failed to leave behind
the reason why she
travelled so
far.

Please others for your
pleasure, please yourself
in spite of others.

Simultaneously she'd be
weeping tears of happiness
from one eye and tears of
sorrow from the other.

People love as much as they
know how to love, the
exceptional few will
always find
more.

One could reasonably
unhappily live with being
considered a 'tortured
genius', but 'difficult
untalented loser' would
be considerably more
bruising to digest.

Happiness is being covered
in spots and boils and
then realising that whilst
hurrying to get dressed
one has put ones skin
on inside out.

As one ages, 'happy' is to
treat others, 'happiness'
is the knowledge of
having done so.

Sometimes I've had so much
fun that I've been utterly
intolerable, people would
travel from far and wide
just to disarm me.

Having been stoned on cloud 9
means I've no recollection
of clouds 1 to 8.

Make him laugh and he'll be
your friend. Make his wife
laugh and he'll be your
enemy. Make his children
laugh and he'll take
a DNA test.

At times I've been so joyful
that I wish there'd been
more of me.

When it comes down to it,
I have enough ups to put
up with the downs.

Original Artwork: Gary Bryon Pateman

ARTISTRY

Creativity is the wings to fly
and the force with which
one hits the ground when
they malfunction.

A self-portrait should also
show what one possesses
on the inside.

Romanticise back to
the day when a box of
paints could spark
a revolution.

I dance like a jangly spasm
that's trodden
on a nail.

Digital abstract art is
mélanging pixels in a
sealable freezer bag
before shaking them
back onto the screen.

We all long to be
the creative
we're not.

The problem with some of
my early paintings is that
their descriptions were
far more impressive
than the paintings
themselves.

Apparently bread is
expensive because it's only
flour and water, an original
Picasso is even more
expensive and it's
only paint and
paper.

Art is creation, risking the
unknown, closer to
fornication than
replication.

A 'work of art' merely
loosens the shackles,
whereas a 'masterpiece'
momentarily removes
them altogether.

Denying oneself creativity is
poisoning the medicine that
would ultimately heal
the frustration.

Art critic's views of
greatness are handicapped
and essentially flawed
by ego.

Artistry is the confidence
to hang a blank canvas,
artlessness is feeling
the need to
decorate
it.

Picture framing borders on
the sublime to the
ridiculous.

Some artists either excel
with their limitations or
camouflage their
inability with
abstraction.

A portrait of a friend should
reveal their true identity,
a portrait of a lover
should not.

One cannot successfully
photograph
music.

Art is attempting to scale a
mountain of inadequacy
in the knowledge that
few if any, ever
reach the
summit.

Why a portrait of that
pervert was ever painted is
beyond me, it isn't only his
eyes that follow you
around the room
but his hands
as well.

Short of creative
inspiration? Just observe
in excruciating detail any
square foot of nature and
the abundance of treasures
that lie therein.

I've just finished some
mouth-watering
designs for
a gourde.

My literary limitations are
due to a l'academia.

If one is constantly satisfied
with one's works of art,
one isn't doing it
properly.

Because of its potential to
be anything, anywhere and
everything, everywhere,
art cannot and should
not be defined.

Painting by numbers is
clipping the wings that
motivate the passion
to pioneer.

Give a monkey enough
time and it'll build the
Hubble telescope, write
symphonies and put
a monkey on the
moon.
(Hasn't it?)

Many an artist has
disappeared up their
own backside with 'creative
block', and many an artist
would rather be no
place else.

Artists paint to be
temporarily free from
torment, unaware that the
act of painting itself, can
be the tormentor.

Creativity is inventing two
notes, not copying note
for note the complete
works of Beethoven.

Hotel lobby paintings are
considered artistic
prostitution.

If one is fortunate enough
to stumble upon a eureka
moment, embrace it with
an enigmatic smile as
one's journey is
about to
begin.

Somewhat ironically,
I used to play music on
Paddy's day in a duet with
one of the snakes Saint
Patrick drove out
of Ireland.

Original Artwork: Gary Bryon Pateman

ECLECTIC

Amputation is cheap, it's the
prosthetic limbs that
cost an arm and
a leg.

If one pleasures in
massaging Greek cheese
into one's private parts,
one may potentially be
considered a fetachist.

Fringe sincerity is
negotiable in pursuit of
popularity.

The parchment is thirsty,
inkwell arid, plume
restless.

Sporting an unusual hat
whilst on holiday shouldn't
end the moment one
boards the flight
home.

Being a lowly crazy paving
slab isn't all it's
cracked up
to be.

When a glider has finished
gliding has it glided
or glid?

During the Covid-19
lockdown we have had
to learn to speak
with our eyes.

One can tell the quality of a
woman by the profundity of
her sincerity, and an old
bag by the integrity
of its zips.

When I'm shown one of the
'sicker' video clips, Mother
Nature discretely whispers
in my ear, reminding me
that I'm trespassing.

The minimalist scrabble
players' next move was
unhampered when his
mind suddenly
went blank.

Clothes pegs generally
come from a long line of...

A spot of spit on your spats
spices them up
like new.

The basis of the Catholic
religion is placing an
irritation into ones eye
and then expecting one
to be eternally grateful
when they remove it.

I organised a survival
weekend and
did.

They call me
wrong beard.

Contrarily, 'higher
and deeper' levels
of comprehension
are both to be
desired.

Doff his cap in reverence?
He'd rather claim to be
completely harmless
than pay homage
to another.

They were as eternally
damned and impermanently
undamned as a schizophrenic
levee.

I spread a rumour of a
rumour which travelled the
entire globe and ended up
tapping me on the shoulder.

I'm not saying that I never
clean the inside of my car
but seagulls follow
it around.

Only poke your own eyes
out if you're certain that the
invention of artificial eyes
will become available
yesterday.

Isn't 'society' simply the
largest of all the
cults?

A 'creative' block is silently
beating one's own
brow.

Acting expressions requires
preparing the desired
interpretation just behind
ones face before performing
it to the outside
world.

Joyless Riders.

The premier requisite when
making invincible glue is
that it must be
vincible.

For the moment I have no
tattoos, those who seek
my opinion can just
ask me.

I've either got an
ingrowing toenail
or an outgrowing
body.

She knitted naked, oblivious
that the offending scarf
would end up 65% mohair,
35% pubic hair.

Reality isn't whether the bus
arrives early, on time or
late, it isn't even
the bus.

It isn't the certitude with
which one expresses one's
opinion that renders it
worthy of an ear.

Modern documentary
makers; they can't all be
the 'toughest prison
in the world'.

People with poor eyesight
have never been able to
read what's written on the
arms of their spectacles
apart from backwards.

Covid-19 has restricted
the number of visitors to
see the 'Treasures of the
Golden Pharaoh' to less
than 3 at any one time,
so only Two-can-come-in.

Original Artwork © Gary Bryon Pateman

DOMESTICITY

During adolescence,
misdemeanours are
invariably one's own
fault as one is both
the perpetrator and
the victim.

Do those who insist on pitch
blackness at bedtime,
sleep with their
eyes open?

Her behaviour was esoteric
to the point of extinction.

Like a motorway levy, a
lifetime of chasing one's
father down the road in
search of recognition
never stops taking
its toll.

Parenting is liberating the
remarkable from the un.

It is short-sighted parents
who don't see further
than their own
children.

Her family possess a portfolio
of silences to rival any
interrogation.

Unideal adolescents ideals
rebel against their unideal
parents ideals, ideally
idealising their
ideologies,
but don't.

Her mere presence
would curdle
milk.

Provide one's children
the option of a superior
education, to travel further
and to fly higher than one
seemed, deemed or
dreamed possible.

Immediately afterwards
I had to look up what it
meant, when my parents
proudly proclaimed that
'for my age, I had a
particularly good
vocabulary'.

If I didn't push the tide back
from time to time, I'd be
dominated to the point
of decimation.

When one refuses to listen,
one equips ones children with
the same obstacles one
has failed to overcome
oneself.

To be snored at is to
be punished for a crime
one hasn't committed.

Parenting is about forgiving ones children for what one previously deemed unforgivable.

She's both cynically inane and clinically insane.

Her inner peace is being absolutely sure in the knowledge that she knows exactly what she's stressing about.

Her mother's rejection is
slow, calculated and
all consuming like
creeping ivy.

The easy part of being a
parent is up until your
children become you
and you become
your parents.

For her, 'chilling out' is the
vindication that her
rage is justified.

As an adolescent I was
encouraged to fly the
nest without having
fully developed
wings.

Most couples are
realistically as compatible
as the strangers they
discover each other to be.

Curiously we are both too
good for each other and
deserve better.

I am no longer strong
enough to continue to
share the burden of her
fractured childhood.

I draw on reality as my
witness particularly during
religious debates and
domestic disputes.

Refrain from being an
'in-a-minute' parent,
when your child wishes
to engage with you.

Every ill proportioned cut
of the cake is like mother
intentionally twisting
the knot in her
throat.

Parents can only claim to
be wiser if they accept
that they're
not.

Sentimentally she's a
safebox with the solitary
key locked inside.

Part of being a parent
is finding ways to accept
the unacceptable, lest we
forget that we have all
fallen foul to similar
temptations.

I've known my mother a
little longer than she's
known me and my
father a wee bit
longer than
that.

Many husbands see an
albatross when the mirror
reflects a turkey and many
wives see a turkey when
the mirror reflects
an albatross.

How often did our parents
remind us that there were
children more fortunate
than us?

Mum has been like a
mother to me.

Original Artwork© Gary Bryon Pateman

ANIMALS

A horse only becomes a
zebra after staring at
an escalator floor
for 30 seconds.

I do not dream of being
anyone else as a horse
doesn't dream of
being a donkey.

Spiritually I'm about as wild,
savage and untamed as a
basset hounds outstretched
apologetic paw.

I bought an ex-customs
dog with a special nose, to,
amongst other things, find
dope down the back
of the sofa.

The greatest grey, bun
munching jazz singer ever;
Elephants Gerald.

I refuse to buy an organic,
0% msg, free range chicken
when it's evidently had a
better life than I've had.

Does a sausage dream
of being a pig or a
hotdog?

Even as an *English* ant, 'I'll
put the kettle on' makes
me incredibly
nervous.

Why would one rather drink
whisky with a thoroughbred
horse or a trusted spaniel
than with a rabbit
or a duck?

I'd like to grow old with all
the majesty, grandeur and
nobility of a hand crafted
ivory chess set. Without
the dead elephant.

If one seeks revenge on
a fly, don't spray it with
repellent, use perfume
and it'll immediately get
rejected by its family,
friends, loved ones and
eventually be forced to
leave the family
cowpat.

Is a crab's peripheral
vision looking
forward?

I can associate as much
with rap music as I can with
a glassblower's dolphin.

Last night mosquitoes took
so much of my blood that
they felt obliged to leave
me a cup of tea and
a biscuit.

Every other living creature
coexists seamlessly with
the landscapes nurtured
by Mother Nature, while
humankind is on its knees
before her, pleading
for clemency.

I lost my dog so I put up
posters of me and the
children as I know he
doesn't recognise
himself.

Is a pigeon tempted to
scratch a key along
the side of a
dove?

Sometimes choosing the
right decision is like finding
an elastic band in a pot
full of snakes.

If a wasp accidentally flies
into the planetarium
does it suffer from
vertigo?

Spiders are generally in
need of a good spin
doctor.

A heartless brigand stole
the legs from under my pet
duck and left it sitting
on a house brick.

Why am I the last bird to
leave the cage yet the
first to close the
door behind
me?

Life has become a bit
gnarled and tatty, like
next doors dog has
been at it.

Dolphins get good press,
sharks get lots of press
and whales couldn't
care less.

Being bitten by a mosquito
in the morning should be in
direct contravention of the
Geneva Convention.

Mosquitoes, never have
I intentionally landed on
you, attempted to suck your
blood or made high pitched
noises in your ears. Please
afford me the same
courtesy.

Animals pass their time
feeding, fighting, fornicating
and filming it courtesy of
the National Geographic.
And you thought you
had an interesting
life?

She effuses the debris of
her past like the plumes
of a decaying
swan.

Under a full moon where
wolves are out to
getcha!

Choosing a coffin is as
irrelevant as a chicken
choosing whether to be
cooked on the BBQ
or in the oven.

If mankind wiped itself out,
would the remaining chimps
evolve and rebuild civilisation
to exactly the same point
as when mankind wiped
itself out?

To see wild horses,
silence is too loud as words
need not be spoken, their
gloriousness, magnificence
and splendour, impassion
enlightenment in a time
long forgotten, yet
desperately
yearned.

Original Artwork © Gary Bryon Pateman

ANXIETY

I'm claustrophobic once
boarded, agoraphobic once
airborne and cherophobic
once landed.

I'm as fed up as a large
toenail during the nail
clippers strike.

For a while I lost my mojo,
but eventually found it
hidden under a pile
of anxiety and
uncertainty.

Anxiety can be the killer
hiding in an imaginary
closet.

I feel like I'm naked,
covered in cooking oil and
trying to climb my way up
from the bottom of a red
funnel, in front of the
whole world.

Only look back at precious
memories from a
stable footing.

Both anxiety and
exhilaration could fit
between the bread of
the same sandwich as they
are equally fuelled by the
temporary abandonment
of control.

Reminiscing with friends
brought home how panic
attacks have shaped past
events when I've not
felt strong enough
to confront the
beast.

I'm a paranoid contraryist
which means that I'm
convinced none of
them are out
to get me.

Panic is opening Pandora's
box and releasing 'what if...
what if... what if...'

When stress fails to respect
our inbuilt limiter, without
fumbling, it passes the
baton to panic.

Whispering one's troubles
multiplies the severity
of them.

I became a potholer in the
hope of joining 'the mile low
club' because of my
fear of flying.

I've spent so long in the fog,
I'm now convinced that
on the other side of
the fog, is more
fog.

Outwardly I'm seething
at the injustice; inwardly I'm
crumpling like a structurally
impaired wedding
cake.

I'm currently taking a
course of placebo's
to counter act the
nocebo's.

My tongue will often throw
itself at the mercy of my
teeth to self harm.

I can live without love and
logic but not without
fondness and fancy.

A panic attack is an
overwhelming acceleration
of negative thought
processes that scare
the hell out of any
rivalling optimism.

Depression is a hat
fashioned from an anvil and
a pair of lead boots.

I bought her some
'electroconvulsive therapy
gift vouchers' in the hope
of downgrading her
psychopathy to
merely psychosis.

Self neglect propagates the
neglect of others.

I don't know if the pessimistic
chapters in this book
are why I wrote it or
because I wrote it.

Striving towards unchartered
heady lows.

I wish to return to nature
to see if I really belong,
everything has become
so alien that I cannot
even find my feet, let
alone a foothold.

She blunders from lake to
lake in search of one deep
enough to drown her
sorrows.

A bad trip is being terrified
that you might have to
continue being you
until it's desists.

Anxiousness is visiting a
prison for those convicted
of having a sweet tooth
wearing only a thong
made of sugar paper.

When one is disappointed
with oneself,
who is?

Beams of happiness
struggle to navigate the
dense, hermetic brume
of darkness.

The arc of anxiety is a
gradual downward curve
right up until the moment
of freefall.

It's only when one
categorically hits rock
bottom that one realises
one is truly alone.

I can feel so unattractive
that if I tried to seduce
myself I would end up
throwing up and locking
myself out of the
bathroom.

The idea of putting
money aside for a rainy day
while living in a monsoon
is as futile as saving your
favourite shoes long after
your legs have been
amputated.

THOUGHTS OF A COMMON MAN
21ST CENTURY THINKS
YOUR QUOTES AND GET THEM PUBLISHED! SEND IN

Λ SELECTION OF YOUR QUOTES

Below is a selection of just some of the quotes sent in to the QTC (Quote Tales Community). When I have received a sufficient quota I will design and publish a book such as this, exclusively for your quotes.

I don't want to go to heaven because of so many of the people that tell me they are.

Gareth
Limerick, Ireland

Thank god it's only arthritis and not the whole thing.

Bryon
Maldon, England

Even though I cannot understand what it must feel like, I understand that we should never feel that way. Therefore it cannot be said that my opinions are dictated purely by emotion, but rather by reason.

Lili
Lille, France

The earth is not ours to trash and burn. We are merely passing visitors.

Jennifer
Walthamstow, England

My dear friend, I wish to be buried before you.

Jean
Saint Lambert la Potherie, France

To give with a good heart is a two way pleasure albeit your time or a smile.

Ann
Frinton-on-Sea, England

I only eat lettuce now because no food expert has said it isn't good for me.

Allan
Frinton-on-Sea, England

In a city with no horizon, there is only sky, an impossible yet infinite landmark to comfort a hive of wandering souls.

Hector
Paris, France

Love is clearing up after an incontinent partner. No it's not, it's disgusting.

Gareth
Limerick, Ireland

To hold another's gloved hand is to share the comfort.

Ann
Frinton-on-Sea, England

If I go to sleep high enough, I can make peace with the noise of the cars driving by, as they suddenly echo the sound of a slow distant tide.

Hector
Paris, France

Mother Nature rises slowly from her slumber, and observes with sleepy eyes in disbelief. She stretches out her endless arms of love, nurture, and repair. And she breathes.

Jennifer
Walthamstow, England

Who first thought of touching mouths to invent the kiss?

Basile
Montpellier, France

If only experts were really 'expert', what a better place the world would be.

Allan
Frinton-on-Sea, England

Thank you and please keep sending them in!

contact@thequotetales.com

OTHER TITLES BY
GARY BRYON PATEMAN

The Quote Tales

Proverbs of a common man

GARY BRYON PATEMAN

THE QUOTE TALES O

PROVERBS OF A COMMON MAN

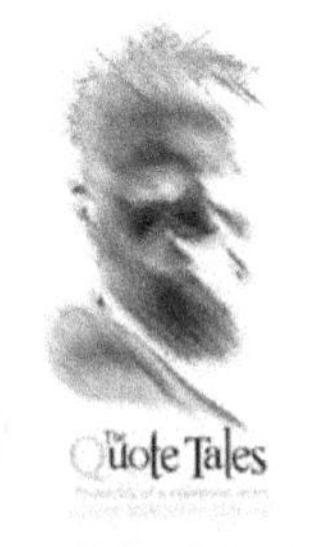

Edition Noir
500 original proverbs
15 original artworks
Pages: 210
Size: 21,6 x 21,6 cm
Content: colour

Edition Noir
500 original proverbs
15 original artworks
Pages: 210
Size: 14 x 21,6 cm
Content: colour

Edition Blanc
500 original proverbs
15 original artworks
Pages: 210
Size: 14 x 21,6 cm
Content: black & white

GARY BRYON PATEMAN
THE QUOTE OF MANY COLOURS

THE QUOTE TALES I
PROVERBS OF A COMMON MAN

Edition Joseph
500 original proverbs
15 original artworks
Pages: 210
Size: 21,6 x 21,6 cm
Content: colour

Edition Joseph
500 original proverbs
15 original artworks
Pages: 210
Size: 14 x 21,6 cm
Content: colour

Edition Joseph
500 original proverbs
15 original artworks
Pages: 210
Size: 14 x 21,6 cm
Content: black & white

21ST CENTURY THINKS

500 ORIGINAL THOUGHTS OF A COMMON MAN

THE QUOTE TALES II

GARY BRYON PATEMAN

THE QUOTE TALES II
THOUGHTS OF A COMMON MAN

Broken Edition	Broken Edition	Broken Edition
500 original thoughts	500 original thoughts	500 original thoughts
15 original artworks	15 original artworks	15 original artworks
Pages: 230	Pages: 230	Pages: 230
Size: 21,6 x 21,6 cm	Size: 14 x 21,6 cm	Size: 14 x 21,6 cm
Content: colour	Content: colour	Content: black & white